FBC: Family Business Circle
Creating Generational Wealth, Using the Money You're Already Spending

By Terrance Amen

Published by
T VENTURES LLC
3145 Geary Blvd # 747
San Francisco, CA 94118
ISBN: 978-0-9847572-0-6

Table of Contents

Part 3: The Family Business Circle

Acknowledgement and Dedication

I would first like to thank the Creator for giving me life and a healthy mind to accomplish the goals I set out to achieve. I know life is about lessons that will enable me to grow in all areas of living. I would like to thank the authors of the many books and courses I had to read and take to help me change my mindset in order to reprogram myself for financial independence and success in the other areas of my life. I dedicate this book to all the individuals and families who have and are struggling to become financially independent. My goal in this book is to lead you in the right direction to fulfil your family's financial goals.

Introduction

Congratulations, this may be one of the best decisions you've ever made in your life, and I truly mean that! You've taken a major step towards becoming financially independent for you and your family, and after reading this book, you'll understand why. Let me say at the beginning, this is not a "get rich quick" book but a family business blueprint to financial success. This book allows you and your family to max out your potential when it comes to financial independence. You may not become wealthy, but by following this plan, you and your family will eventually become financially independent. Whether you're young or old, make low five figures or high six figures or more, this book is for you.

It depends on how serious you are and how far you want to go with this information. It also depends on how much money you have to start with, which is why it's so important to get your family members involved. You do realize that whenever you work for someone, you're being paid less than what you produce, right? This is capitalism at its finest. The owner can't pay you what you're worth because if they did, they wouldn't make any profit from all that you produce, which is why they pay you less than what you produce. So, the solution is to work for yourself or even better, start a family business.

Starting a family business allows you to multiply your efforts in order to achieve financial independence in the shortest time. This is a small book, but it gets right to the point, full of simple but powerful methods you and your family can take advantage of in order to begin your journey to financial independence. This information has been around for a long time. Unfortunately, it's not taught in schools. We're not taught how to make money, only how to work for it and how to spend it. After reading this book, you'll never be able to say you don't know how to create financial independence for you and your family using the money you're already spending.

Once you have a foundation of learning how to build wealth, you'll have a variety of ways you can use to create financial independence. But you don't have to go it alone. The bigger opportunity is coming together with other like-minded family businesses in order to create a network of opportunities that your family business can capitalize on. Believe it or not, it's not difficult to become financially successful. There are stories about people who only made minimum wage but were able to become financially successful. They had the knowledge, a plan, and they took action. It wasn't easy, it took a while, but it was done. Always remember, big things take time, and financial independence is big!

So why do so many families never reach the level of financial independence? They don't have the right mindset or a solid plan on building wealth, and they are afraid of taking action. Going to college to get a good job, investing in a 401k, and working forty years to retire is what most of us are taught and what we believe is the way to financial independence. A lot of times they're going it alone, which makes it even harder to accomplish your financial goals. It's not to say it can't be done, it's just harder and takes a lot longer.

Therefore, I'm focusing on families working together in order to achieve their financial independence. You'll be able to succeed much faster by working smarter, because you're already working hard. I consider you family, so I'm going to say some things you may not agree with or like. Let's just call it tough love. Here we go. Some of this you may already know, and you may want to skip to other topics. Please don't. You may miss out on some really good gems. This book is small but packed with information that has the potential to change not only your life but your family's life as well.

Hang in there with me because I guarantee you: by the time you reach the end of this book, you'll be glad you didn't skip sections. At the end, you'll see in the reference section how hard it is to become financially independent, especially going it alone. But if you have the right mindset, a solid plan, and you work together with your family and take action, you can achieve your financial goals in a shorter period of time. The ultimate goal of having a family business is to be able to live off the interest of your investments while never touching the principal. This is one of the main reasons why the wealthy stay wealthy. The interest comes back every year from the principal, and they continue to build on it. This won't happen overnight, but with the right plan included in this book, you and your family will be on your way to reaching your goals of becoming financially independent.

Part 1: The Problem

The Government

Part of the reason it's so hard to become financially independent or wealthy (they both mean the same to me) is because of wages. Our wages haven't kept up with inflation and worker productivity for a very long time. If they had, the federal minimum hourly wage would be in the twenties or more (Luhby, 2021). Think about that for a minute. That's why you hear the term "living wage" used a lot. It means we're not making enough to keep up with the cost of living, with everything going up except our wages.

The federal minimum wage hasn't gone up since 2009 (Luhby, 2021), but everything else has. It's harder to save money to invest when you only make enough for living expenses. Remember, a lot of people are doing this by themselves, which makes it that much harder. If you're married, you have a better chance of achieving financial success because you have two incomes to work with rather than one. But it's still hard because of the wages and lack of the right knowledge. Even people who have good incomes are struggling because of the cost of living, student debt, insurance, housing, etc. You get my point. So, it's the government's fault, right? This leads us to the next chapter.

Politics

Who is the government and why are they going against what's best for us? Well, the government is who we elect to represent us. So why aren't the people we elect representing our best interest? Because they don't have to, based on us voting for the same people every two to six years. How do you hold them accountable if you keep voting them in every year? You can't, which is why we must stop voting for the lesser of the evils. They're both evil. Both parties are controlled by big business and the wealthy. But we have more power than them: voting power! Unfortunately, both parties know how to keep us divided, which is why we vote against our own best interest. We all want the same things: a government that's fair, that protects us, and that works for all of us and not just the few.

The powers that be know how to play us against each other. What am I talking about? Religion, race, class, and sex are the biggest issues. So, what's the solution? If we voted based on policy and what's best for our country as a whole, rather than what's best for us as individuals or our group concerns, we could solve this problem. We're not going to get everything we want based on our personal wants, but we can get what's best for all of us. Vote for someone who has your best interests in mind based on policies. If they don't do what they said they were going to do, vote them out. It's just that simple. I could go into more details, but this book is about building family wealth and not politics. I just wanted to say something about this because of how important it is to not only your family's success but our country, as well.

Taxes

If you didn't know, taxes are one of the biggest obstacles to becoming financially independent. Why do you think the wealthy and major corporations fight so hard and spend billions to keep their taxes down? They know taxes cut into their bottom line. Unfortunately, we don't fight as hard or spend billions to get Congress to lower our taxes, or at least make the wealthy and corporations pay their fair share. So, if you can't beat them, join them in a better and more principled way. What do I mean by this?

We're not trying to pay no taxes at all like a lot of the wealthy, we just want to lower our taxes as much as we can so we have a better chance of becoming financially independent. Taxes do serve a purpose; they fund the things our city, state, and federal governments use to keep our country running right. Unfortunately, this isn't working with our schools, roads, water systems, and anything else you can think of that needs to be fixed. Part of the problem is that the wealthy and major corporations don't pay their fair share, but you do.

If you added up your city, state, and federal taxes, it may come to thirty percent or more of your income. That's a big hit and a major obstacle to you and your family becoming wealthy. The only way you pay less in taxes is if you're poor, which you never want to be (that's the reason you're reading this book). The poor pay little to nothing in taxes because they make little to nothing in income. If you're wealthy, which is where you're headed if you follow the plan in this book, there are ways you can save and pay less in taxes.

Corporations are set up as they are in order to raise money and save on taxes. You and your family can take advantage of this setup through having a small business. Having a business is a great way to cut down on your taxes. Having a family business is a greater way to cut down on not only your taxes but your family's taxes. This will allow you to reach your financial goals that much faster. Once you realize this most important point of this section, you can focus on the mindset, which will help you focus on having the right program.

Mindset

This section is probably the most important part of this book. If you don't have the right mindset, nothing else will work. It took me many years to understand this. But no matter how old you are, it's never too late to develop the right mindset. Life is about the program. If you have the right program, you'll become successful in your life. If you don't, life can become a living hell. The program most of us are in is the "get a good education, so you can get a good job" program. Then we work forty years in order to retire comfortably. What a sad program, yet this is what the majority of us do every day, and we pass this mindset down to our children and grandchildren.

If you look at many of the most financially successful people in American history, they either didn't go to college or they dropped out. Now I'm not against going to school. There are obvious advantages, especially if you're learning a trade or profession or if you have love for a certain field like teaching, social work, nursing, etc. But if you're going to college just to get a better job, this may be a problem when it comes to building wealth.

The data bears this out because of the debt many put themselves in. You're not guaranteed to make enough money to live a comfortable life because of the cost of living and how long it will take to retire, and you probably won't become financially independent (Tretina, 2022).

Okay, I think you get my point, which is why you're reading this book, right? I just wanted to remind you. Now let's talk about a financially independent mindset.

People with this mindset think outside the box. They do the opposite of what everyone else is doing. This is how the wealthy think, and they pass this mindset down to their children. This is how they create generational wealth. Their businesses are set up so all family members can contribute to and benefit from them. However, most family members in average families work individually rather than working together as a family, which makes things harder than they need to be for everyone. Some family members do work together but don't create a family business to capitalize on all the available benefits.

Another key point is instant gratification. We're programmed to want things instantly rather than waiting until we have the funding to buy them, which is why the country is in big-time debt. An example of this is the trillions of dollars we spent in wars, which we still will have to pay off from our taxes. Do wars benefit us, or do they benefit big business? Most people don't think about these things, and this is one of the reasons they don't achieve financial independence.

You have to develop the mindset of long-term gratification rather than instant, at least in the beginning of your journey to financial independence. But this won't take as long if the family works together. It may take a generation or two to achieve wealth, but by planting the family business seed, you will see results in a short time. Now you understand why I say this is not a "get rich quick" book. If you don't change the instant gratification program, you probably won't become financially independent, or it will take you a lot longer to achieve it. By reading this book, you're already ahead of the game.

Fear

This is part of the mindset section, but I felt it was important enough to have a section of its own. Believe it or not, many people have the knowledge to become successful, but they let their fears get in the way. What fears am I talking about? Fear of failure, fear of loss, and believe it or not, fear of success. What I'm about say next is so important that once you understand this, you won't ever let fear stop you from accomplishing your goals, no matter what they are. Are you ready? Here it goes: is fear doing something or is it the thought of doing something? Read that again. As Franklin Greenwald once said, "Do what you fear, watch it disappear" (Greenwald, 1989).

This means is that the fear is not in doing it, because once you've done it, there's nothing more to fear. The fear is thinking about doing it. Read that again. That's why it's so important to have the right mindset. Your thoughts are very powerful. They can help you succeed in life or stop you from ever trying to accomplish your goals. Make sure you get this program down. This is so important to having a successful life, let alone having financial success. It determines how far we go in life. You could be on the verge of success but are afraid to take that next step because of fear. Just by taking another step, you would have determined if you're ready to go to the next level.

You might get introduced to a business or investment opportunity that could change your life but are afraid of what you may lose or what other people may say if you fail. These are not good reasons. A key part of life is making the right choices and taking certain risks. It's unavoidable if you want to be successful. You should weigh the pros and cons. In my opinion, if you have a fifty-fifty chance or better, go for it. We walk past opportunities every day, but if you don't change your mindset of fear, you'll never see them or act on them even if you do see them.

Trust me on this. I had to learn this the hard way. It's not fun looking back on opportunities you could've taken but didn't for fear of failure or loss. It's not fun struggling in life when you had the opportunity to be financially independent. This happened to me because I didn't have the right mindset. But I knew something was wrong with the way I was thinking. I started reading books on overcoming fear, on odds, on positive thinking, and anything else I could find to help change my mindset. Working smarter is learning from other people's mistakes. You don't have to waste time and money. Instead, learn from my mistakes and the mistakes of your parents, grandparents, and their friends.

We've been taught and programmed that we live in a world of limitations, which is why we're so fearful of change. In reality, we live in a world of un-limited potential. The people who think this way don't see limits; they only see unlimited potential. This is why such people are the most successful, while the people who only see limits are the least successful. Having the right mindset to overcome your fears is very important to your family's financial success.

Health is Wealth

You can have all the money in the world, but if you don't have good health, how are you going to enjoy your financial independence? I consider us family, so it would be wrong for me to not talk about good health and how to achieve it. The stats are horrible when it comes to our health in the U.S. Here are some stats from the Centers for Disease Control and Prevention (CDC) that should make you want to think about focusing on your health. According to the CDC, 6 in 10 Americans have a chronic disease. 4 in 10 adults have two or more. The main killer diseases are heart disease, cancer, chronic lung disease, stroke, Alzheimer's disease, diabetes, and chronic kidney disease (Murphy et al, 2021).

The main causes of these diseases are tobacco use, poor nutrition, lack of physical activity, and excessive alcohol use (Murphy et al, 2021). If you take out the hereditary factors, a lot of these diseases can be prevented and maybe even cured. So, stop smoking and cut down on your drinking. If you can't do that, you really shouldn't be drinking. Start exercising and eat as close as you can get to a vegan diet. If you can't do that, eat the least amount of processed foods, which I believe are the major causes of these diseases. Remember, it's all about the mindset.

Once you have the right mindset, everything else will take care of itself. Just like changing your program to becoming financially independent, you have to change an unhealthy program to a healthy one. You can't focus only on your financial independence and not focus on your health. They both work together. How? Well, you have to be able to think outside the box, and that takes a lot of energy because you're going against what the unfortunate majority of people do. This includes your own family. That alone takes a lot of energy. Trust me, I know. I've been a vegan for over thirty years and have been telling my family that this really works.

Now I must admit, I'm not in the best shape I could be in, but based on my age and family history, I don't have any of the major killer diseases that I mentioned above. I consider this to be because of my vegan diet. Unfortunately, some of my family members do suffer from some of these diseases. Okay, I've said my piece on this. I just wanted you to know the importance of being healthy on your journey to financial independence.

People will try to tell you the family business won't work, our family won't work together, we don't have any money to do this. You're going to hear all the excuses for not trying this, and it takes a lot of energy to counter all the negativity you're going to hear. But one thing is guaranteed: you won't achieve the goal of financial independence for you and your family if you don't try. That's guaranteed! So, you're going to need a lot of energy to counter and move past the old programs. This is why it's so important to focus on your health while focusing on your family's financial independence. We only have so much energy in a day, so use it wisely. Work smarter because you're already working hard. Okay, let's move on.

Part 2: The Solution

Three Major Ways to Become Wealthy

Okay, I've talked about the problems; now let's get to the real nitty gritty. There are three major ways to become financially independent: having your own business, investing in real estate, or investing in the stock market. If you combine them all, that creates a fourth way to maximize your family's wealth potential. These four ways are the foundation of wealth building. There are other ways, but these are tried and true.

The first way to build wealth is owning a business. If you don't have a business, then you're not fully taking advantage of what this country has to offer. Remember, this is a capitalist society and most if not all the benefits go to businesses, big and small. Here are some examples. Believe it or not, you used to be able to write off your credit card interest. Not anymore. Now only businesses can do that. If you own a business, you can write off most of your business-related expenses, which, if you're still working, can offset your taxes on your job's income. That's really a big one, considering how much money we pay in federal, state, and local taxes every year.

The second way to build wealth is buying real estate. This is what most families use to build wealth because of the many benefits to owning a home. Homeowners also get tax benefits. But most homeowners buy a home to live in and not really to invest in. Over time, it can become an investment because of the equity that builds up over time and can be passed down or used for funding your child's education, home improvements, high-interest debt consolidation, an emergency fund, buying a car, a vacation, a wedding, along with many other uses.

The third way to build wealth is investing in the stock market. This is how many people have obtained their wealth. Believe it or not, it's the wealthy that own the majority of the stock market. The idea is to buy a stock that goes up over time so you can cash out, borrow against it, or live off the dividends. That is, if the stock goes up.

The Family Business

If you can't help your own family, who can you help? Right now, you're making everybody rich except your family. In an environment in which wages haven't gone up in decades, you have to find other ways to build wealth. The wealth gap is bigger than it has ever been, including the Gilded Age, and we're contributing to it (Telford, 2019). That's where the family business comes in, where you can begin to level the playing field by bringing some of the money you spend outside your family back to your family. By creating a family business, you will not only help your family but other family members for generations to come.

You will be educating future generations on what to do with their money so they don't have to think about what to do with it. They already will know what to do and why to do it. When you have a family business, you multiply the speed, money, and success of your business. Your family business has the potential to lower your taxes and give you the ability to hire family members. Most importantly, it will allow you to create generational wealth for your family. This is what farmers have been doing for generations: saving on taxes, hiring their family, and passing down their wealth. Instead of having a farm, your family business would have a finance and investment company.

I know, I know, you don't get along with your family, family members owe you money and they can't take care of their own finances. This is why they need to read this book, to understand how important it is to work together as a family in order to achieve financial success by having a family business. There will always be reasons not to create a family business, and you may not be able to work with some family members. That doesn't mean you throw the baby out with the bath water, as the saying goes. I'm pretty sure you can find some family members who are responsible and professional enough to want to work together with you. This may also motivate the other family members to want to get their act together in order to be a part of this.

This is so important because of the many benefits of having a family business. How do you think some of the wealthy got started? They got help from their family and built on that to where they're at now. They either got help from their family or started a family business. If it's good enough for them, it's definitely good enough for you, right? Once your family sees the benefits of having a family business after reading this book, I'm pretty sure you'll have some relatives that will want to participate. Other than working together in business, there are not a lot of ways you and your family can become financially independent.

The risk of starting a family business is low because you're sharing it with more than one family member. I'm also going to show you how to use the money you're already spending to get started, so there's very little risk, if any. You and your family really have nothing to lose and a whole lot to gain creating a family business. One person can only do so much, but a family working together has the ability to solve a lot of financial problems. How much money you start with may determine how long it takes. As I said earlier, this is not a "get rich quick" scheme. It may take a generation or more, but you'll see the benefits right away and be glad you started the family business.

The sooner you start, the sooner you'll get to financial independence. We've been taught to go to college in order to get a good job, then work forty years to retire in order to reap the benefits of our labor. But who really reaps the benefits from our labor? The employer benefits immediately while you wait forty years, and you still might not benefit. According to data the Social Security Administration and the CDC, many people retire between ages 62 - 70, (Social Security Administration, 2022) but the average life span for men is 77 and the average for women is 81 (Murphy et al, 2021). So, you may work 40 years to enjoy only 13-19 years of retirement.

This is average, so you may get lucky and live a little longer or shorter, which, again, is why it's so important to take care of your health.

This is not to say you won't enjoy some of the time in between when you start working to when you retire, it's to show that you can do much better for you and your family. You don't have to reinvent the wheel. Just follow the strategies of other successful people. Most importantly, if you want to maximize your potential to create wealth for you and your family, starting a family business is one of the best ways if not the best way to do it. Imagine trying to create wealth by yourself. How long do you think it would take, if it is even possible? Now imagine multiplying yourself with other family members working together with you to achieve the same goal.

There are going to be some families who hit the ground running with this information because they have or make enough money and just need a solid plan to implement in order to take action. Unfortunately, there are going to be some families who won't even try to use this information, but no matter how long it takes, don't give up on your family and its future.

If you add up all the reasons why you shouldn't start a family business, it won't come close to all the reasons why you should start one. Ask yourself: is what you're doing now going to lead to the things you want in life for you and your family, and if so, how long will it take? In life, we all have to make choices that will not only affect us individually but will affect our family as well. Don't be left behind when you have an opportunity to become financially independent by working together with your family. After all, who's more important than your family?

Next time you have your family reunion, the concepts presented in this book should be one of the major topics. Actually, these concepts would be a great reason to have a family reunion. Whether you have a family reunion or not, you'd only need to meet once a week in the beginning and maybe once a month to check on the progress and what can be done better after you have everything in place.

Okay, I've said enough on this subject. But remember, these concepts regarding starting a family business are major keys to building family wealth in the shortest period of time.

Family Unity

You can't have a family business without the family. There are many reasons why you should have a family business, but if the family is not united, it will be very hard to become financially independent in the shortest period of time, if at all. One person can start a business and benefit from the information in this book. But to really capitalize on this information, you have to do it together as a family. I'm going to intentionally be repeating myself throughout the book in this specific area because it is the key to your family's financial independence and happiness and deserves the most attention.

We have not been taught to work together to create financial independence in the family. This is not to say families aren't doing this, it's just not how we were taught to become financially independent. We were taught to do things independently. Don't get me wrong, we work together out of necessity or when it's convenient, but not having a solid plan on how to work together as a family to achieve financial independence is a major reason why families continue to struggle.

Not working together is a key issue that doesn't allow the family to maximize their financial goals. Let's focus on some reasons why you shouldn't have a family business and see if they outweigh the advantages of working together to have one.

The family is scattered across the country

With today's technology, there's no reason why the family can't work together to form a family business. You can pick the state where most of the family members live and set it up there. But it still doesn't matter because once you set up the business, you can add the family members that are participating in it, no matter where they live. Making family members aware of the family business is a great purpose for a family reunion. You can also do this remotely with the different live video services. Meeting remotely is not the same as coming together in person, but it still can be done in order to discuss creating or expanding the family business.

Family is not reliable

Unfortunately, this can be true with some family members, but that's no reason not to set up the family business. You'd be surprised what a family member will do to change their behavior when it comes to creating a family business that will benefit them and the whole family. The family business can be set up so the members can contribute automatically through their bank. Making or saving money can be a great motivator for the unreliable member to change their behavior.

Family members don't get along

Once you set up the rules and obligations of each family member who participates in the business, it really doesn't matter if a family member doesn't get along with others. Remember, the family business will benefit all family members that participate and, to a certain degree, even those who don't. What's more important is that every family member realizes that by supporting the family business, each of them will benefit as well. The benefits will provide great incentive to want to participate. It's a matter of changing the mindset to working together, rather than working individually, in order to achieve the same goals of financial independence.

A family member owes money to other family members

Where there's a will, there's a way. There's a way in which a family member can pay back what is owed and still be able to support the family business. Part of the revenue made by the family business can go to the family member that is owed. Remember, you're putting the family in a position to creating generational wealth. So, don't focus on the small stuff when the bigger picture is what's most important. The key is to get started because the sooner you start the family business, the sooner the family will see the benefits of having one, the sooner you'll reach your financial goals.

Family can't be trusted

This is a very important point, which is why I left it for last. You must be able to trust your family members who join the business in order for this to work. As I said earlier, having a family business where all the family will benefit in one way or another is a great incentive for family members to do the right thing. This may be a new concept for the family and a great way to make amends for past issues. This is a personal matter that you and the other family members have to confront, but don't let the past slow your future success and be the reason why you don't try to do the right thing. Remember what the big picture is: the goal of the family business is to create financial independence and generational wealth.

Lastly, when the family expands through marriage, so does the family's financial success. If the new family doesn't have a family business set up, you can show them through your family's business the potential for even more financial success. This will encourage the new family members to join your family business. This is what they used to do in the old days and is why wealthy families would only marry into other wealthy families. But it can be done with families who aren't wealthy yet. With the right mindset, you're creating a family that works together to create financial independence. Remember, the more family members you have dedicated to the family business, the more money you'll have for the business, and the sooner your family will become financially independent.

Benefits of Having a Family Business

- Having a family business multiplies the speed, money, and success of your business
- The ability to save on taxes
- Financial independence
- Educating and preparing future generations
- Creating generational wealth
- The ability to work for yourself
- You can pay your family more or less in wages
- No classism, racism, or sexism
- You won't get laid off
- The ability to hire your family
- You can be yourself
- Very little commuting
- The coffee and food are better at home
- You can do personal things while working the family business
- You don't have to quit your job to start a family business
- You're working with your family
- Unlimited income potential
- Setting your own schedule

- A lot of flexibility
- You can buy in bulk

There are many more benefits that I'm sure you and your family can add to this list.

How to Raise Money for
Your Family Business

The first step to raising money for the family business is for each family member who is participating in the business to set up a budget for their finances. This way the participants know where they may be able to find places they can cut back on expenditures or where they can cut some of their expenses. An example of this is needs versus wants. You need food, shelter, transportation, clothing, etc. These are necessities. But you may want an expensive car, watch, shoes, or to dine out three days a week. By cutting back on your wants, you'll be able to find some of the money for your family business.

If you don't have any extra money, how do you begin? Well, there's always a way if you want something bad enough, and this is worth finding a way for. If you get a tax refund every year, you are basically giving the government a loan, and you're not getting any interest on that money. By changing your W2 form, you can get more money in your paycheck. That money can be used to begin raising money for your family business. If you have a savings account along with a checking account, you can use the savings account to start your family business.

It makes no sense to earn one percent or less in the bank when you can use that money to earn more by starting your own family business. Now imagine if you can get other family members to do the same. Then you will have something to work with. Another way is getting a part-time job just to raise the money you need to get started. How about getting a roommate or moving into a family member's home for a set period of time until you've raised enough money to start the family business? If you have children already living at home, you can charge them rent at a discount and put that towards the family business, which they'll benefit from in the long run. Basically, you would be doing an Airbnb with your family.

Another way is using credit or equity in yours or another family member's home. You may be able to get a better interest rate by using equity rather than just getting a loan or credit cards. Remember, this is for the family business, so you can write off the interest on your taxes. Be careful though because the goal is to get out of debt, so make sure you're getting the lowest interest rate possible.

To summarize: ways to raise money include budgeting, changing a tax form, using your savings account, working a temporary job, getting a roommate, or moving into a family member's home; another way is to use home equity or credit.

Remember, in life, we all have to make sacrifices. Who better to sacrifice for than your family?

The key is to make that sacrifice count in order to accomplish your family's financial goals. The sooner you set up your family business, the sooner you can begin to take advantage of all the benefits of building family wealth in the shortest time. By working together with your family, you cut the time it takes to reach your financial goals. Keep that in mind when you're deciding to work with your family or not.

Pay Your Family First

The concept we are going to discuss here is a takeoff of "pay yourself first," famously illustrated in *The Richest Man in Babylon* by George S. Clason. Let's consider this concept with the family business in mind.

You often hear in conversations about personal finance about paying yourself first, but what does that really mean? When you have bills to pay including rent or mortgage, car, utilities, food, clothes, entertainment, which one do you pay off first? The answer is in the title of this section: pay yourself first (Clason, 1930). I'll be using pay your family first for the rest of this section.

What this concept does is let you know what you can afford even before you buy anything. Of course, this concept can be applied more easily by the youth because they don't have all the bills and debt older adults have accumulated over the years. So, by teaching this essential concept to your children and grandchildren, you will plant a seed that will steer them to pay themselves first by saving and investing when they start receiving money, including allowances, money as gifts, and anything else that they do to bring in income. Savings should be thought of here as saving for future investments.

The sooner your family starts, the more money the family will be able to save and invest.

This concept still applies to mature adults, although it may be harder because of the bills and debt they may already have. This will still work because family members will be using a budget that will allow each member to know what they can afford to contribute to the family business. For example, when family members get a raise or a money gift, they can use part or all of this new money to put away for the family business before they use it for anything else. How much each member chooses to pay the family first would be determined by how much each can afford to save. Whether it's $100, $1,000 or $10,000 a week or month, pay your family first!

Now if you're using money to pay off debt, once that debt is paid off, you should make payments of the same amount to your pay your family first account. This is the difference between a young person with no debt and someone that has accumulated debt over the years: it's very hard to save for investing and pay off debt at the same time. It can be done but it's not a good way because of the interest rates you pay every month on your debt.

By focusing on eliminating debt before paying your family first, this will free you in the future to save on interest payments and add that money to the family account. Just remember to use the money you were using to pay off the debt to instead add to your pay your family first account. It's all about maximizing time, effort, and money.

Setting Up Your Family Business

Before I get started in this section, I am not a lawyer or accountant, so when setting up your family business, please consult with a lawyer and accountant for the best way to set up your family business. Each state may have different laws regarding the different entities. If you don't need to raise any new money for your family business, congratulations! You're already that much closer to achieving your family's financial independence.

It is very important to set your family business up the right way. It shows you are taking this seriously and are professional in your actions. Also, when you have family members involved, you want to make sure you have everything in writing so everyone knows their roles and what they each are bringing to the table. The business can last in the family forever.

Each family member can make a commitment to investing $100 or more a month to the family business. You can do this automatically by setting aside the amount you choose to contribute to the family business through your bank. No matter how much money you can contribute, the key is to start where you are. Take action!

There are different business entities to set up your family business. One common example is a C corporation. This is what big businesses use to raise money and eventually sell shares to the public. An LLC is what most small businesses and even some big businesses use in order to protect their personal assets from lawsuits. S corporations also have advantages as well. According to Investopedia's "What Is an S Corp," an S Corp can have as many as 100 shareholders and can pass taxable credits, deductions, and losses through to those shareholders (Kagan, 2022) Then there's the sole proprietor, but I don't suggest this one because you have no protection from being sued and you can lose everything you worked for. I suggest using an LLC, at least to start. You can have as many family members as you want. You can elect family managers who can oversee the family business.

You can also make the business democratic, where the family would vote on setting up the rules of the family business and on what opportunities to pursue through the business. It doesn't have to be one hundred percent agreement of the family voting. You can have a majority, or whatever percentage you want. You can have the family managers vote. It's all up to you and your family, which is why LLCs work for a lot of small businesses. Once you've talked with your family and received legal and tax advice, you can decide what entity to choose from. Now, let's talk about some strategies to making money for your family business.

Using the Money You're Already Spending to Create Financial Independence

In the beginning of having your family business, you want to be as conservative as possible. You don't want to take risks in the beginning because it can set you back in accomplishing the family business goal, which is to become financially independent in the shortest time. So, in the beginning, you want to act like a bank. Banks rarely take risks, which is why you rarely hear about banks going out of business. This is not to say they don't, it just rarely happens because of how they're set up.

Let's say you have family members in debt. The family business can pay off that debt, and the family will be able to get the interest that would be paid on that debt rather than an outside company. After all, they're already paying on the debt, so why not pay it to the family business? Does that make sense? Now of course you're not going to charge your family the same interest that was paid to the company charging the interest, but you can cut the interest in half. That's a win-win for the family business and the family member in debt. The family member repaying debt can also invest part of the interest savings into the family business. There's no extra money needed other than the money you're already spending or saving for the family business.

Here's another example of how to use the money you're already spending to accomplish your family business goals. You have three family members who are in credit card debt. One owes $10,000, the other $5,000, and the last owes $1,000. Which family member's debt do you pay off first? Most people would pay off the highest debt first or the debt with the highest interest rate. But that may take the longest time and use the most money because of interest accruing on the debt. If you paid off the lowest first, that would take the shortest time to pay off and is the least amount of money to raise.

So, the family business can raise the money to pay off the principal of the $1,000 debt in a lump sum, and contract with the family member to repay the business with a lower rate of interest than they would have owed the credit card company. Once the smallest debt is paid, the family business can work with the other two family members in debt in a similar manner. When the last debt is paid off, the family business would be able to keep the interest payment that would have gone to the credit card company on the that last debt. Now you can use that repaid $1,000 to help pay off the $5,000. Now the family business only has to raise an additional $4,000 to pay off the $5,000. Once that's paid off, the business now has $6,000 to pay off the $10,000 while earning interest for the family business.

Do you see a pattern here? Your family business would not be using any extra money; it will be using the payments provided by family members in debt while keeping money in the business that would have been interest for the credit card companies. By this method, the business can pay off family debt in the shortest time and strengthen the family by removing debt as a concern for the individual relatives. In the long run, this would be a powerful investment in the interests of the family, and therefore for the family business. Make sense? This is called maximizing time, effort, and money. These are key examples of how your family business can raise money and generate interest revenue for the business while getting family members out of debt at the same time.

Now once your family members' debts are paid off through the business, it doesn't mean they go back into debt. The goal for your family business is to buy everything through the family business and pay it off through the business, which allows the business to pay all future debt off in the shortest time while earning interest for the family business, using the money the business already has to pay it off.

Now the money goes to your family business rather than an outside business. By doing this, you're turning family liabilities into assets. Start small and build with the money you're already spending. Start with the smallest amount of debt and work your way up to the highest. You're basically becoming a finance company for your family. Think about how much interest you've paid to companies, then multiply that by each family member. It adds up to a fortune. By just capturing that interest, you can get a great start to your family's financial independence in the shortest time.

Whether it is credit cards, car loans, mortgages, college loans, or anything else, you pay interest on those loans. Now think about how much money the family business can make on these loans. You can apply this to any type of debt.

Let's say one of the family members wants to buy a car. The family business can buy it and charge less in interest than what it would cost the family member if they were to buy it on their own. A win-win for the family member and the family business.

Remember, you want to give your family a reason to want to go through the family business for these loans. The family business can lease the car to the family member or buy it outright. Whatever is best for the family member and family business while earning interest on it is what the family business can set up. The family member would be paying the interest anyway, but because they lease or buy it from the family business, they save money through a lower interest, and that interest is going to the family business instead of an outside company.

How about student debt? Well, the family business can pay for a family member to go to school for what the family business needs, not just to get a good job.

How about a house? Once the family business has enough for the down payment, the family business can buy the first house and rent it out to a family member until it's paid off while being able to write off all the expenses attributed to it. If one family member can afford to buy a house on their own, imagine what a family business of three or more relatives can do.

What if no family member can afford to buy a house? Together, a family business of three or more relatives may be able to. This should be the goal of the family business, because every family member may want to buy a home, car, college education, etc.

Remember, the ultimate goal of a family business is to get to the point where you can live off the interest that's made from the principal and to never spend the principal. When you get to this point, your family has made it to financial independence.

Want to lower your family's food cost? Buy the food from a Costco or other discount food companies with your family business credit card and sell it to your family at a five to ten percent markup. Now you can also get the Costco membership in your family business's name. Remember, this is a business, so you have to charge more than what you paid for the food. You probably could charge quite a bit more, but you don't want to overcharge your family. Many families can't afford to buy in bulk because they don't have the space; your family business can solve that problem for your family.

You can also separate the food and deliver it to your family members. Remember, it's your family business, so even though you're charging a little higher price, it goes back to your family. Also, you bought the groceries at a discount, so the cost could be less than regular retail prices or, at the very least, you could break even. Buying low and selling high is the foundation of a business, and you just created a family food store and delivery service. Family members can tell you what they want to order, and you buy low and sell a little higher and deliver it to them. You just created a two- to four-hour part-time job for a family member once or twice a month. Once the family business can afford it, you don't have to charge a higher price for food.

This is just another way of using the money you're already spending in order to generate revenues for the family business account. You can also hire your family members to do things you would have had to pay someone outside your family to do, and if they need to take a course or classes in the different areas, guess what, that's a business expense.

We have elders in our families who need help getting around. You can hire a family member to become a home health worker, driver, or cook. Since the elders may be the most established and will need help in the future, they should be made a priority. They may also be the ones to help fund the family business because they may have equity in their home but are not sure how to use it.

These strategies can also be applied by the family business to childcare and anything else you can think of. This way, the money stays in the family and can be used to lower your family's expenses while generating revenues for the family business. Once the family business becomes financially independent, you can pay to send a family member to school to become an accountant, doctor, or whatever the family business needs. This is what wealthy families do, so why can't your family do the same? Some of the savings can go towards funding your family business.

Another example is your home. You're probably saying, I already have a mortgage, so how can this strategy help me? Certain mortgages can be transferred to a new owner, and if you have such a mortgage, you can transfer the mortgage to the family business. Remember, the goal is to have everything in the family business, so you can turn a family member's property into rental property for the business. This allows you to write off all expenses having to do with the property while the family member still lives there and pays rent to the family business. The only difference is the family owns the property together, and the business pays the mortgage. This allows the business to write off all expenses of the property because it is now an income property.

You can also buy a home for each family member this way with the family business. The family business will benefit from the rent coming from the family member and from the value of the property while also generating assets for the family business and saving on real estate taxes.

Your family has nothing to lose setting up a family business and financial independence to gain. Now some of these things may take some time to apply, but you'll be surprised how fast this will work once you get started. Remember what I said in the beginning: this is not a "get rich quick" book but a family business blueprint to your family's financial independence.

Your success will build momentum to motivate your family business members to find as many ways as possible to fund your family business. The key is getting started. The sooner you start, the sooner you'll see results, the closer you'll get to reaching your financial goals. You're also teaching young family members the benefits of working and contributing to the family business. This is what the wealthy do to keep the money in their family. Wealthy families rarely spend money outside of their family circles when they don't have to, and your family can learn to operate the same way. Remember, it's all about the mindset.

Now, are you ready to accelerate your family business into overdrive? Instead of one family business member making payments towards their debt, other family business members can contribute to paying off that family member's debt using their monthly contributions so the business can pay off that debt faster. This multiplies the speed with which the debt is paid off, allowing more funds to be available sooner to pay off the next debt or other investments. The goal is for the family business to become financially independent in the shortest time, right? Doing it this way will get you there in the shortest time.

Emergency Fund

It's very important to create an emergency fund for your family business. The Covid-19 pandemic proved how important it is to have one. You can take part of the revenues from your family business to build up the fund. You can also buy insurance for the family business. Remember, you want to use the money you're already spending to start with. It is said that it is best to have at least six months to a year in reserve, in case of an emergency. Since this is a family business and you have family members contributing, I would lean towards a year or more.

Emergencies happen in life. It's always good to be prepared for them. The saying goes: it is always better to have money and not need it than to need money and not have it. Once the family business has the emergency fund for the family in place, it can focus on generating more revenue for the family business. Remember, some of the revenues the family business receives can go into building the fund. This way you're not using your personal money but the family business money, which you'll be able to write off. This is called working smarter, because you're already working hard.

Talk To Your Family

If this information makes sense to you, buy or share this book and start talking to your family about it. You may not get all your family members on board, but you may be able to get some members on board. By the time you finish this book and explain to them how this works, you'll be able to get a lot more on board. Once they see the success of the family working together, the rest will get on board. Make sure you talk to the elders, their children, and their grandchildren. Remember, you're working on building generational wealth, and each generation can bring something to the table.

The elders have wisdom from their experience and may have the funding to help get the family business started. Their children are living the current experience and should be able to contribute, and their children can tell you what the latest new things are and are able to do the running around. They also have more energy you can use to get things done. It also gives them an incentive to want to be more involved in the family business.

The bottom line: no one knows everything, and the more you all contribute, the more support you'll get, and the faster you'll succeed in accomplishing your financial goals.

This is key to the family business growing. If you don't work together, you make it that much harder for your family to succeed. You can start a model business as a family member to show the rest of your family how this works, or you can do it as a family business with a hundred members. The more family business members, the faster you'll achieve your financial goals. After all, what family member wouldn't want to cut their interest rate in half while supporting the family business? This should also help family members raise their credit score.

There are too many benefits to not set up your family business, so like Nike says, just do it! Even if a family member doesn't want to work in the family business, they may still want to get a better interest rate on whatever they're buying.

Pro Athletes & Entertainers

(Before we start on this section, this also applies to high-net-worth family members who are not athletes or entertainers.)

Athletes and entertainers can utilize this family business plan to help their family while saving on taxes and expenses over time. Instead of just giving money to the family, they can set up a family business and fund it, allowing those family members who participate to utilize the business the same way they would a bank. They would be able to borrow from the business to save on interest while paying that money back, and this would build revenues to sustain the family business for generations to come.

Athletes and entertainers can finance and build a family business that can buy everything the family needs through the business, and the business can then generate revenues and save on taxes. This is a great way for athletes and entertainers to help their family help themselves while still building financial success for the family's future. This is how the wealthy have been doing it for centuries, so it only makes sense to do the same thing.

A lot of pressure is put on athletes and entertainers to help their families, and rightfully so because often, they are the bread winners but probably wouldn't have been so successful if it wasn't for their families. The best way for athletes and entertainers to continue to support their families is to set up a family business, because their fortunes from their careers do not last forever. Many times, they end up broke, which is sad because it doesn't have to be that way. If they utilize the family business model, they may not have to worry about that anymore. The primary goal of a family business is to be able to live off the interest while never spending the principal. This is true financial independence, and it is as available to athletes and entertainers as it is to everyone else.

Financial independence should be the major focus of every family member who joins, supports, and contributes to the family business. Over time, things get a lot easier because you have a lot more funding to do more for the family. At the beginning, the initial focus should always be on generating revenue for the family business while saving on taxes. This can be a win-win for athletes and entertainers and their families. Remember, big things take time, but the support of family members who are already financially successful gives your family business a big advantage over other families that have to start from the beginning by raising money for their family business.

(I also have a plan specifically designed for athletes and entertainers. Contact me on familybusinesscircle.com for more information.)

Giving Back

To whom much is given, much is required. This is just a reminder to show your appreciation for what you have by helping those who don't have as much. I've found out in life that things don't always happen when you want them to but when you need them to. This is based on a natural or universal law that says when you give, you'll receive. If you think you can become successful and have a happy life without giving back, you will find out the hard way it doesn't work like that. It's a fact that you can become financially successful, but your success will not be complete until you give back. Whether to your church, alma mater, or a favorite charity, giving back shows your appreciation for the things you have.

Even if you're not where you want to be yet, it's always a good idea to help those who could use your help. Whether it's some kind words, helping someone who could use your help, giving change to a homeless person, or whatever, it's a good idea to help someone who's not as fortunate as you. Of course, this starts with your family, but not just your family. Helping your family is already expected and is a natural process, but to help someone you don't know, a total stranger, is a very powerful physical, mental, and spiritual gift for not only the person you help, but for you as well. How do you think that person feels after you've helped them? You could have saved their life or prevented them from doing harm to themselves or to someone else. It's a domino effect that keeps giving in many different positive ways.

In my opinion, giving back is what's missing in this world. Not enough people are giving back because of greed, lack of money or resources, a scarcity mindset, or are only focused on their immediate circle and concerns. This becomes a domino effect in a negative way. People remember how they were treated, both the good and the bad. Negativity breeds more negativity. Positivity breeds more positivity. Even if there's a negative situation, it can be at least neutralized by a positive response, and often, a positive response can change a negative situation for the better.

Think about it yourself and how you felt from the positive situations you've experienced as compared with the negative ones. If you received a positive experience, you're likely to pass that positive experience on. But if it was negative, you may pass that experience on to someone who doesn't deserve it. After all, we're human and go by our emotions and how we've been treated. So, remember this when you experience a positive or negative situation. If it's negative, end it with that specific situation. If it's positive, it's only natural to pass that feeling on to someone else.

I didn't mean to go on a long speech about how to treat one another, but I thought this was so important that I couldn't leave this out. Now, let's get back to the big picture, and I mean big picture!

Part 3: The Plan --
Family Business Circle

The Plan

As you can see, this is not rocket science. It's having a different mindset, changing from relying on the government and jobs for financial resources to adopting a plan that maximizes your family's potential for financial independence.

I wrote this book for two reasons. First, I wanted to show you the simplicity of creating wealth once you have the right mindset, a solid plan, and are ready to take action. Second, I wanted to introduce you to Family Business Circle, or FBC. Remember, you can do a lot more with two family members than one, and so on. Now imagine a network of family businesses working together to become financially independent. Let me introduce you to FBC.

Family Business Circle

As you read in the solution part, there are only three major ways to become wealthy: a business, stock investments, and real estate. FBC will offer these three ways and much, much more. You may already have your family business set up. If you don't, this can be one of the ways FBC can help you and your family. Imagine being able to save or make money on almost everything you buy, and you own the company. Part of the revenues will come back to your family business when someone you refer signs up and buys the products and services at FBC.

When the company grows in value, so does the value of the shares you own. Family Business Circle (FBC) is a business opportunity created to educate families on how to start a family business that includes financial education, paid referrals, investing in FBC, and real estate investing. This is done by monetizing the products and services you're already spending money on. One example is legal advice. When you have a business, you should have legal advice at the ready whenever you need it. A lot of businesses don't have this service because they think they can't afford it, but working with FBC, you'll be able to. There are prepaid legal services you can use now, and FBC will be creating or buying an existing company to provide this service to our members.

When it comes to taxes, it's always good to have a tax advisor go over or, even better, do your taxes. They can also represent you if you ever get audited, at a discounted rate of course. For another example, the big banks always find ways to get more money from you without giving you anything in return. This won't happen at a bank you own and can generate revenue from when a family member or someone you know signs up for an account. For another example, if your family members are looking for a mortgage, they won't have to worry about not getting a loan based on the class they are in or the color of their skin if the family business buys the property for them. Whether each relative personally has good credit and can afford the mortgage matters less; since the family business is buying it, this gives each relative a better chance of getting it. The same process would go for car and any other type of loans your family business may need.

Examples include cell phones and plans, banking, insurance, and more.

Here's a list of other opportunities:

- Farms
- Airlines
- Cruise lines
- Travel agencies
- Real estate agencies
- Real estate development
- Hotels
- Car dealerships

Opportunities are available in many other fields as well. I think you get my point. The benefits of becoming a member of FBC is that you'll be able to save or make money on the products and services used while owning a piece of these different industries and receive commissions from them when someone you refer signs up and uses a particular product or service.

It would be very hard for your family business to do this on its own, but together in FBC, your family business and the other family businesses that are signed up (or that you sign up) can receive revenue that you wouldn't normally receive. The lack of this business revenue is one of the reasons for the wealth gaps between the classes. You also may benefit from the rise in your shares price. This is how you can close the wealth gaps and bring some of the billions spent outside your family back to your family. You're basically supporting a startup in its earliest stage.

At the time of this writing, FBC is in the friends and family stage. What does that mean? We're on the ground floor and first stage of the investment ladder. This is the riskiest stage but also has the most potential. We're not set up yet for you to invest directly, which is why we're asking for a small donation or for you to buy a few books to give to your family and friends. You'll eventually be able to invest in FBC, which covers the stock investment part of the three ways to becoming wealthy. You only need one stock to make a ton of money in the market. Just imagine if you had invested early in one of these companies like Microsoft, Amazon, or Apple. You would be rich or, at the very least, comfortable.

Your family business can sign up other families and receive commissions on the products and services they buy. This is a way to bring likeminded families together to build family wealth in the shortest time. I'm talking about family power! No corporation on the planet can compete with a circle of small family businesses working together.

Remember, the majority of businesses are small businesses. But they don't work together, which is one of the reasons they stay small. In the corporate world, small businesses merge with other small businesses to gain market share. This is what FBC was created to do. Working together with FBC can also give you more political power. This is how major corporations, and the wealthy get what they want from politicians. Together, we can do this too. This isn't rocket science. It just takes the right mindset, a good plan and action. You won't be in this by yourself. You'll be united with other like-minded family businesses. If you like this book, and believe in this plan, here's a way you can make a small donation that will help FBC get set up in order to maximize your family's wealth potential in the shortest time.

Making a small donation now will help FBC build a website and backend service for setting up network marketing software, *but not multilevel marketing*. It's been proven that multilevel marketing doesn't work for the majority of people who join, but just for the company and its top sales reps (Tarver, 2022). FBC only has one level, which allows for more money going directly to the individual family businesses and is a better business opportunity for more interested people. Families will be paid from referrals when someone becomes a member and buys the products and services they use, including expanding and automating products and services including legal and accounting services.

FBC will have experienced executives to help run the company, marketing, and the process of going public on the OTC exchange. This allows us to save money on the cost of going public while family business members can potentially make more money instead of venture capitalists, and the public will be able to buy and sell shares in the shortest time. Once we generate enough revenue, we can go on the major exchanges if it makes sense to do so. Investing in FBC can be like investing in multiple major industries without having to invest in them individually. Talk about maximizing time, effort, and money!

By doing this, you can cut the risk down because, remember, your family business and the many other family businesses who sign up are already using and buying in these different industries, so all are making sure FBC will be successful. This keeps the money circling back to your family business and FBC. For example, when FBC is set up to offer these services for new members, they'll be able to set up their family business using FBC's legal services to help them set up their business and whenever they need legal help. Your family business will receive a commission from those you sign up. They're going to want tax help, and when they do, your family business will receive a commission on that and whatever else they buy or other services they use.

That's why it's so important to help FBC get up and running. The sooner FBC is set up, the sooner your family business can start making commissions on products and services that most people are already using. The goal of FBC is not to sell you stuff you don't need, but to build from the revenue created from your purchasing of things you're already spending your money on. The goal of FBC is to have products and services comparable to or better than the products and services you're already using. This is what I'm showing you through this book: how to create wealth using the money you're already spending.

Benefits of Supporting and Becoming a Member of FBC

If you and your family are not ready to go it alone yet, you can take advantage of the many services FBC will have to help you transition to a family business. FBC is being created specifically to help create revenue for your family business.

If your family business is low on cash, you'll be able to generate revenue by helping other family businesses. Your family business will receive commissions when you refer other families to FBC and they sign up and buy products and services.

FBC will have a system in place to help your family business promote and market the plan to potential FBC members. This book is an example of a promotional tool.

Your family business will be able to create multiple streams of revenue.

Your family business will be able to invest in FBC while generating revenue from the products and services offered by FBC.

Investing in FBC is like investing in multiple different companies, which lowers the risk of FBC failing and increases the opportunity of your family business succeeding because your family business and the other family businesses will be buying and using FBC products and services.

FBC will offer products and services you're already using and services that will help you keep the wealth you've attained, including tax planning advice, family trusts, foundations, etc.

As an FBC member, your family business may be able to benefit from discount volume buying, which lowers the price when you buy with other family businesses.

As an FBC member, your family business will be able to generate monthly commissions on all the products and services families use every day that you wouldn't normally be able to access as an individual retail customer.

FBC includes the three major ways to become financially independent as quickly as possible, so your family business doesn't have to look anywhere else. FBC will have products and services families are already buying that you can make commissions on. Your family business will eventually be able to buy stock in FBC, and eventually your business in cooperation with others within FBC will be able to develop and/or buy real estate.

Network Marketing

I put this part after the FBC part so that you could see the potential in supporting and eventually investing in FBC. This is very important, so don't skip or get upset. Network marketing gets a bad rap because of the way it's used, but used properly, it can be all the positive things it was meant to be. Unfortunately, most network marketing companies are set up for the success of the company and the major sales reps in the company. In my opinion, network marketing simply means you're marketing a product or service or both to people you know. Whether it's family, friends, or coworkers, you're simply marketing to them.

The problem, in my opinion, lies in multilevel marketing, which is far different from network marketing. In my opinion, multilevel marketing is more of a payment structure rather than a way to market because you need to have the network part first. Network marketing has been around since before modern businesses were created. A new business starts with marketing their product or service to the people they know. This is only natural because the business owner knows his or her circle of family, friends, and coworkers will be supportive. After all, if you had a business, wouldn't you start with the people who know and trust you first? They know you wouldn't try to cheat or rip them off, which is why they'd want to help you get off to a great start.

But when you add multilevel marketing to the mix, multilevel marketing changes everything because of the way it's set up. In my opinion, this system is not set up to help the vast majority who participate in multilevel marketing because the system may charge more than what the product or service would normally cost. These companies may also pay many different levels to many different people in order to justify charging the higher prices. So, for you to make good money, you may need to recruit a ton of people. The problem lies in the cost of the product or service and in how many people you may need to recruit to make a decent amount of money.

This is why multilevel marketers have to focus on making money from recruiting rather than the products and services. It is said that just recruiting new members is a pyramid scheme, but this is what salespeople get paid to do, whether it's for a product, service, or new employee. The problem is these are professionals or people who have the gift of gab, but most of us are not natural salespeople.

I'd like to introduce you to a new way to use network marketing, the way I believe it was meant to be used. I'll end this chapter with this: the Family Business Circle only has one level, and our focus is on selling competitively priced products and services, along with recruiting new members.

Benefits of Network Marketing

- A turnkey system
- Low startup cost, low risk, potentially high reward
- Word-of-mouth advertising is better than commercial advertising, because you know and trust the person telling you
- Work with people you want to work with
- No employees needed
- Residual income
- Great business for women
- Work from home or anywhere
- Tax benefits
- Save money
- Proven business model
- Network marketing levels the playing field
- No education requirements
- Low to no overhead
- You're able to multiply your family businesses money and efforts.
- Your family business will be able to make commissions on products and

services, you wouldn't normally be able to.

- Network Marketing enables your family business to work part-time.
- You can earn residual income through the efforts of others you sign up, not just your own family business.

Time to Take Action

You know the problem, you know the solution, and you now have a plan. By following the information you've read in this book, you'll be able to start a family business and eventually become financially independent. But why go it alone when you can work with other small family businesses and, together, potentially reach financial independence that much sooner? You would have to do the same things going it alone as you would working with FBC. The difference is you'll be able to invest in FBC.

Through FBC your family business will have multiple ways to generate revenue, like investing with other FBC members to invest in FBC stock, real estate, products, and services. You can start as a family business of one or one hundred. The key is to get started. Take action! I hope you're excited about your family's future. Now you have a reason to be. This is not rocket science, this information is not new, but is a way for family businesses to work together to maximize their potential and become financially independent.

This is the future of business. A functional example of the freedom this can create for individuals is the gig economy, but we're taking this to a whole different level because family businesses are going to own the company and receive commissions from every product and service FBC sells. Many industries will become automated, using artificial intelligence to save money for their companies. This will impact many individuals in the gig economy, but you can get ahead of it by forming a family business and teaming up with other family businesses to grow market share. You have very little to lose and a whole lot to gain.

This isn't a pipe dream; this is what the wealthy and families who farm have been doing for centuries. They hire their family, save on taxes, and create generational wealth for their family. Now it's your turn. Rather than having a farm, your family business will generate its own finances, and also can use FBC as a store and an investment company.

With the knowledge you've received from this book, your family business can go it alone and still be very successful. Over time, you'll eventually become financially independent. But why take the slow road and go it alone when you have more opportunities to be financially successful working with other family businesses? You'll have multiple ways to generate revenue by helping other families achieve their financial independence. You'll be able to promote products and services and own a piece of different industries that sell products and services that families use every day. By working with FBC, you'll have the potential to get to your destination of financial independence a lot sooner.

It's always harder when you work alone, but by working together, there's very little that can stop you. The risk is lower while the rewards are greater. By working with FBC, you cover the three major ways to becoming financially independent with one company: starting a family business, buying FBC stock, and buying and investing in real estate through FBC. This is how corporations get started and grow to multibillion-dollar companies.

If you keep doing the same thing with your time, money, and family, you'll keep getting the same results. Don't you think it's time to do something different in order to get a different result? By working with FBC, your family business will not only own the company but will be able to earn commissions on the products and services FBC sells. Not too many companies can say they were created to bring billions back to families. This is why it is so important to support a company that will offer you these many opportunities for your family business to succeed.

FBC is not going to be a company that just takes; its goal is to help those families who need help to get started. By helping families, FBC will help itself, your family business, and our country. FBC is about creating win-win solutions for everyone involved.

Bottom line, you can continue to do what you've been doing by working and struggling individually, or you can start a family business and reap the benefits of working together in order to become financially independent in the shortest time. Consumer spending is what makes this country run. Right now, the majority of that money goes to major corporations and the wealthy. But by family businesses working together, we can bring some of those trillions back to the family, which will lower wealth inequality and create a happier nation.

This is not just a book on how to create wealth for you and your family. This book also offers you a potential business and investment opportunity. I say "potential" because this plan depends on how much support I receive from you and your family to build FBC. I'd rather receive support from you to build FBC than get a venture capitalist involved. Venture capitalists want to control an entrepreneur's company, and if they don't like what you're doing or you're not making money fast enough, they can kick you out or demote you. This happened to Steve Jobs, one of the founders of Apple. After he left, the company eventually went down. Now keep in mind this was a very successful company that had some hiccups, yet they still kicked him out. But the company was doing so bad that it brought Jobs back. As they say, the rest is history.

Now I'm not in position to not accept venture capitalist or angel investors, but they won't like my demands to stay in control of the company, so they may not want to invest in FBC. But their loss is your gain. Please keep this in mind when choosing to go it alone or to work with other families to get what we all want: financial independence. Remember to start where you're at, start small and work your way up.

Let's work together as family businesses to build and expand our circle in order to help our families receive some of the trillions we produce. By doing this, we not only help our families but our country as well. Remember to keep it simple, but whichever way you choose, to go it alone or do both by supporting and investing in FBC, I truly wish the best for you and your family's success. It can be hard becoming financially independent, but with the right mindset, the right information, and a solid plan of action, you can reach your financial goals in a shorter period of time.

If you like this book, please share it on your social media and write a short review while it's on your mind. For independent authors, this is one of the most important steps in helping to get the word out about their books. Please share and write a review now on Amazon or wherever you bought the book. I would greatly appreciate it. Also, here's a list of some of the books that helped me on my journey towards financial independence.

1. *Think and Grow Rich* by Napoleon Hill
2. *The Magic of Thinking Big* by David J. Schwartz, PhD.

3. *The E Myth* by Michael E. Gerber
4. *Rich Dad Poor Dad* by Robert T. Kiyosaki
5. *Debt Free & Prosperous Living* by John M. Cummuta

Thank you for your time.

P.S. For more information, updates, and to make a small donation, please go to familybusinesscircle.com

FBC Bonus Chapter

This section is dedicated to giving you even more reasons to follow the family business plan inside this book and support FBC.

Earlier in this book, I said, "When your family business members buy a house, you might want to consider fully furnishing it, with the approval of the family business member who will be living there. This includes furniture, a washer and dryer, a TV, cable, internet, and any other amenities your family business can provide to make the home suitable for the family business member. All of these amenities may be tax-deductible, and your accountant will let you know what isn't. This is a great example of buying property in the family business as rental property, rather than personal property." The more you buy in your family business, the more taxes you can save. It's just that simple.

Now, are you ready to be amazed? What I'm about to share with you is one of the most powerful financial instrument secrets hidden in plain sight. Here are some examples of what it has in it: it's safe, liquid, offers major tax advantages, allows you to borrow against it for investment opportunities and emergencies, earns compound interest, and is lawsuit-protected. Corporations, banks, and wealthy families use it. Can you guess what it is? It's whole life insurance!

I know some of you are saying, "This can't be right," and the reason you're saying this is that you weren't taught how to use whole life insurance in this way. Most financial advisors will tell you to buy term life insurance and invest the savings that you would have paid for whole life insurance in the stock market. Yet term life insurance is like renting an apartment: once the term is up, you lose all the money you put into it. Who does that benefit: you or the term life insurance company? You would also have to pay more for a new policy when the term expires because you're older, and your health might not be what it once was.

Term life insurance also doesn't have all the advantages that whole life insurance offers. Whole life insurance covers you for your entire life as long as you continue to pay the premiums, and you'll receive all the benefits that go along with it, including the death benefit. I learned a lot about this from reading *Becoming Your Own Banker* by R. Nelson Nash. He actually came up with the ideas for how to maximize the whole life policy to get all the advantages I mentioned above.

Families have been buying whole life insurance for centuries, as I said, but even some of the wealthy don't know how to use it for all the many benefits it has to offer (Nash, 2008). But, using the family business plan along with buying whole life insurance can turbo-charge your family's generational wealth. By using whole life insurance, your family business can get a lump sum of hundreds of thousands or even millions of dollars, depending on how much you have to put in the policy. This is why it's so important to work with your family to accomplish your goals of financial independence in the shortest time using the money you're already spending.

Think about what your family business can do with five hundred thousand or a million dollars — perhaps buy more property for your family business members, invest in more whole life policies for the next generations. They say you shouldn't say guarantee, but done right, a family business with a whole life insurance policy, and a trust to protect your assets is the closest thing to a guarantee you can get to creating generational wealth for you and your family.

Now the key to this is finding the right insurance agent who knows how to set up your policy so that it benefits you first, not the agent or the insurance company. Remember: this insurance plan is a new way of using your policy. It's only twenty-five or thirty years old. That's pretty new, compared to the industry. This is why you should think about supporting Family Business Circle (FBC). So, you'll not only get great products and services, but you'll also have a trusted company that you own a piece of, with benefits including access to educational seminars about the power of whole life insurance and access to trusted, vetted partners who can meet your family's insurance needs.

The bottom line: either you spend your hard-earned money to set up your family business and receive all the benefits that go with having one, or you don't. Once you set up your family business, it has the potential to last for generations to come. Your children and grandchildren won't have to figure out what to do with their money; they'll already know to contribute to the family business. This benefits the whole family. Or you can continue to buy and borrow everything outside your family business and let total strangers who only have their best interest in mind receive all the benefits that could have gone to your family. The choice is yours. Based on the information in this book about all the benefits of having a family business, I think the best choice is clear.

I hope you enjoyed this bonus chapter, and thanks again for your time. Don't forget to write a review on the book wherever you bought it.

References

Clason, G.S. *The richest man in Babylon.* New York City, NY, USA: Penguin Books, 1930.

Greenwald, F. 1989. *Do what you fear, watch it disappear.* Postcard. San Francisco, CA, USA: NoSecretsPress, 1989.

Hayes, L. N. (2017, August 24.) *Living paycheck to paycheck is a way of life for majority of U.S. workers, according to New Careerbuilder Survey.* Press Room | Career Builder. Retrieved October 10, 2022, from https://press.careerbuilder.com/2017-08-24-Living-Paycheck-to-Paycheck-is-a-Way-of-Life-for-Majority-of-U-S-Workers-According-to-New-CareerBuilder-Survey

Kagan, J. (2022, September 25.) *What is an S Corp?* Investopedia. Retrieved October 20, 2022, from https://www.investopedia.com/terms/s/subchapters.asp

Luhby, T. (2021, February 21.) *These two charts show how much minimum wage workers have fallen behind.* CNN. Retrieved October 20, 2022, from https://www.cnn.com/2021/02/21/politics/minimum-wage-inflation-productivity/index.html

Murphy, S. L., Kochanek, K. D., Wu, J., & Arias, E. (2021, December 21.) *Products - data briefs - number 427 - December 2021.* Centers for Disease Control and Prevention. Retrieved October 10, 2022,

from
https://www.cdc.gov/nchs/products/databriefs/db427.htm

Nash, N.R. *Becoming your own banker: the infinite banking concept.* Birmingham, AL, USA: Infinite Banking Concepts, 2008.

Social Security Administration. *Starting your retirement benefits early.* (n.d.) Social Security Administration. Retrieved October 20, 2022, from https://www.ssa.gov/benefits/retirement/planner/agereduction.html

Tarver, E. (2022, July 25) *What is an MLM? How multilevel marketing works.* Retrieved November 26, 2022, from https://www.investopedia.com/terms/m/multi-level-marketing.asp

Telford, T. (2019, September 27). *Income inequality in America is the highest it's been since Census Bureau started tracking it, Data Shows*. The Washington Post. Retrieved October 10, 2022, from https://www.washingtonpost.com/business/2019/09/26/income-inequality-america-highest-its-been-since-census-started-tracking-it-data-show/

Tretina, Kat. (2022, June 21.) *Is college worth the cost? Pros vs. cons.* Forbes. Retrieved October 20, 2022, from https://www.forbes.com/advisor/student-loans/is-college-worth-it/